The Droitwich Discovery

A play

Nick Warburton

Samuel French—London
New York-Toronto-Hollywood

Please see page iv for further copyright information

THE DROITWICH DISCOVERY

First performed by SUDS at Sawston, Cambridge-shire, on 7th March 1996, with the following cast:

Shakespeare	Peter Green
Mrs Craddock	Val Furness
George	Chris Goodwin
Olive	Carol Tomson
Dilly	Lyn Pepperell
Karen	Jean Green

Directed by Ted Sharrock

COPYRIGHT INFORMATION
(See also page ii)

CHARACTERS

Shakespeare, William's brother Terry, who also plays William, Williamus, Baldiano, Kevin

Mrs Craddock, Terry's "landlady", who also plays a Toddler, Portia's assistant and the Reporter

George, who also plays Henry VIII, John Shakespeare, Mr Biggs, the Prince of Majorca and Porker

Olive, who also plays a Toddler and Portia

Dilly, who also plays a Teacher and Portia's assistant

Karen, who also plays Anne Boleyn, Mary Shakespeare and a Barmaid

The action takes place in an attic in Droitwich

Time—the present

Other plays by Nick Warburton published by
Samuel French Ltd:

Don't Blame It On The Boots
Distracted Globe
Easy Stages
Ghost Writer
Loophole
Not Bobby
Receive This Light
Round the World With Class 6
Sour Grapes and Ashes
Zartan

THE DROITWICH DISCOVERY

Music. Lights half up on an attic in Droitwich. It is gloomy and full of clutter—chests, old boxes, piles of clothes, etc. Some of the clutter is placed by the door. As the music fades, we hear voices outside the door

George (*off*) Open it, then. Open it.

Dilly (*off*) I'm trying to open it. It's stuck.

George (*off*) Here, let's put a bit of beef behind it.

Dilly (*off*) No, don't, George. I think we ought to wait for Mrs Craddock…

George (*off*) One, two, three, heave!

The door pushes open, forcing boxes etc. out of the way. A shaft of Light enters, followed by George, Dilly, Olive and Karen

There you are. I said, didn't I? A bit of beef.

Dilly I still think we ought to've waited for…

George Look, we're paying for a Shakespearean tour. We're not paying to stand around on a dusty staircase. You can't afford to let these people shove you around.

Olive Where is she, anyway?

Dilly She said she had to fix a fuse…

George Fix a fuse! We're being had, Dilly. Thanks to you, we're being had.

Olive For God's sake, give it a chance. We've come all this way. We might as well…

The Lighting comes on full. They stand blinking around them for a moment

George Good grief!
Olive Fantastic.
George It's a bloody tip.

Karen puts up a finger to indicate that she wants to say something

Karen George...
George Not now, Karen. (*To Dilly*) You expect us to believe that Shakespeare worked up here? In a bloody tip of an attic.
Dilly Well, it said in the pamphlet...
George Pamphlet!
Olive (*wandering around*) He might've done. I mean, I can just picture him, scribbling away up here.
George I don't believe it. I don't believe they even had attics in those days. (*To Dilly*) You useless tart.
Dilly It's not my fault, George.
George Of course it is. You're the secretary. You were the one who was supposed to book this trip.
Dilly Well, I did book it. I did.
George But Stratford we said. Bloody Stratford.
Dilly Stratford was already booked.
George We were supposed to have a backstage tour and see a matinée. And what have we got? Droitwich.
Dilly I thought it would be different.
George It's different all right. It's a waste of bloody time.
Karen George...
George Not now, for God's sake. Four pound fifty to stand up to our ankles in dust.
Olive Oh, stop moaning, George. You don't know that Shakespeare didn't work here, do you?
George Cobblers!

Olive No, really. I can feel the vibrations. Things happened up here. I can sense it.

George Yes, people brought rubbish up here and dumped it.

Mrs Craddock (*off*) I fixed the fuse. No extra charge.

Mrs Craddock enters and sees the others. She is an unlikely tourist guide, with an apron and an unlit fag dangling from her lip

You found your way in, then?

George Ah, Mrs Craddock. We were just saying, weren't we ladies, how refreshingly different all this is.

Mrs Craddock It is. Not many people know that whassname lived up here.

Olive Shakespeare?

Mrs Craddock What?

Olive Shakespeare lived up here.

Mrs Craddock I know. That's what I just said. (*She clears her throat, disgustingly*) Right. You ready for your tour?

They all nod and make sounds of enthusiasm

OK, then. Whassname—William Shakespeare—came to Droitwich in fifteen seventy-four to take up work here...

Dilly What sort of work?

Mrs Craddock What? Mending drains, I think.

Olive Fifteen seventy-four?

Mrs Craddock Yes.

Olive When he was only ten?

Mrs Craddock What? Yes, well, they went to work young in them days.

Olive But I didn't think they had drains in the sixteenth century. Not as such.

Mrs Craddock gives her a withering look

Mrs Craddock They did in Droitwich. Droitwich was always one step ahead of everyone else. Anyway, he came here—to number forty-one Ellesmere Gardens—where my ancestor, Mrs Elizabeth Craddock the First, gave him bed and breakfast.

Olive Fantastic.

Karen Excuse me, may I ask…

Mrs Craddock Look, are you all going to chip in every two minutes? Because I've got a lot to get through here.

George Don't interrupt, Karen.

Karen Sorry, George.

Dilly Do go on, Mrs Craddock. It's really fascinating, isn't it, everybody?

Mrs Craddock Right. (*Another clear of her throat*) So he'd spend the day digging drains, and then he'd come back here and write all evening. Most of his stuff was done up here. Othello, Whassname the Third, all that lot.

Olive Fascinating. His actual body, up here all those years ago.

Mrs Craddock That's right. Right. Any questions?

Dilly What?

Mrs Craddock Any questions?

George You mean, that's it?

Mrs Craddock What more do you want? I've got another lot to show round soon, you know.

Olive You mean, "This is where he wrote most of his stuff", end of lecture?

Mrs Craddock It's a guided tour, not a lecture.

Karen (*holding up her finger*) I have a question.

George You would.

Karen How did the boxes get behind the door?

Mrs Craddock What?

Karen When we came in there were boxes piled against the door. How did they get there?

George What's this got to do with Shakespeare?

Karen I was just wondering…

George This is wasting our time.

Olive She's got a point, actually.

Mrs Craddock I put them there.

Karen But you'd have to be inside the room to do that.

Mrs Craddock I was. I was inside the room. So, if there's no more…

Karen So how did you get out? Without moving them again, I mean.

Pause. They all look at Mrs Craddock

Mrs Craddock I just did, didn't I?

Karen But how?

Mrs Craddock What is this? *Inspector Morse*? You've had your tour so now you can all bog off.

Olive Oh, that's nice. Very English Heritage, that.

Mrs Craddock You think you know it all, you lot. I tell you all about Shakespeare and you go on and on about a pile of old boxes. What does it matter?

Karen Well, if you moved them, how did you get out? And if you didn't move them, who did?

A voice answers from the depths of the rubble

Terry I did.

The others look round, puzzled

Dilly What?

Terry I said, "I did". So will you now leave me in peace?

Dilly There's someone else up here! George, George do something! (*She clings to him*) There's someone else up here!

George Let go of me, woman. Of course there's someone else up here. That's how the boxes were moved.

Mrs Craddock It's one of you lot, isn't it? You've paid for four and there's five of you.

Olive But don't you know who it is?

Mrs Craddock Not as such, no.

Terry Shakespeare stirs among the boxes and emerges. He is dressed in Elizabethan garb

Terry It was me.

They are stunned

I said it was me.

They stare at him for a second. Then there is instant chaos. Everyone is shouting and overlapping

Dilly There's a man up here! There's a man up here! Do something, George!

Karen The boxes! The boxes! I knew there was something wrong with the boxes!

Olive whoops and runs round the attic, searching the rubble

Olive Fan-tastic. Absolutely fantastic. (*To Terry*) You're so *authentic*. You got anyone else up here? Come out, come out, wherever you are!

Mrs Craddock You paid for four and there's five of you! What do you take me for? Come on. Cough up, will you?

All this goes on for some seconds. Terry stands still in the middle of it all. Eventually...

George (*bellowing*) Calm down, will you! Will you all please calm down!

The panic suddenly stops

There is a very simple explanation for all this. There must be.

Terry There is.

George See?

Terry This is my attic and you're trespassing.

Mrs Craddock It's not your attic. It's my attic.

Terry My dear woman, I've been here nearly four hundred years. I think I can reasonably claim that it is mine...

Mrs Craddock Nearly four hundred years! Nearly four hundred years in my attic?

Terry My attic.

Mrs Craddock At seventeen pounds a night. And you haven't paid a penny. That's nearly two and a half million quid you owe me.

Terry What for?

Mrs Craddock Bed and breakfast.

Terry Rubbish! I don't sleep and I haven't had a bite since sixteen eleven. If you want to play that game, madam, I believe I'm entitled to about one hundred and thirty thousand bacon and eggses.

George That's ridiculous.

Dilly You must be starving. (*She delves in her bag*) I think I've got some shortbread in here somewhere.

George What are you talking about, shortbread? He's been here since the beginning of the seventeenth century. This man is dead.

Dilly Dead?

George Four hundred years? He must be.

Dilly goes into a panic of her own

Dilly Dead! Dead! This man is dead! We're trapped up here with
a dead man!
George Shut up!

She doesn't

Will you shut up! (*He gives Dilly a hefty belt*)

She calms down at once

Listen to me, woman. He's four hundred years old, so he ought
to be dead. Right?

She nods breathlessly

But he's obviously not dead, is he?

She shakes her head

So there's some other explanation…
Karen He's a ghost.
George Of course. (*To Dilly*) He's a ghost. See? (*He panics*) He's
a ghost! He's a ghost! (*He runs up and down, turning this way
and that and shouting*)
Dilly Shut up, George!

He doesn't

Shut up at once! (*She gives him a hefty smack*)

He calms down at once

George Thank you, thank you.

Olive I said I could sense something up here and I was right. He isn't alive and he isn't dead. He's a ghost.

George Right! That's it. I'm off! (*He makes for the door*)

Terry Oh no, you don't. (*He snaps his finger*)

The door slams shut. They all turn to him, amazed

You don't come up here disturbing my peace and then clear off without a word. Oh no.

Karen No, listen. He's right. It's very rude of us. And anyway, this is a rare opportunity. To talk to the man himself.

Mrs Craddock So you do know him, do you?

Karen But haven't you realized, Mrs Craddock? (*To Terry*) You are Mr Shakespeare, aren't you?

Terry I am.

Karen There you are, you see. We can converse with the Bard himself.

Mrs Craddock At a price.

George What?

Mrs Craddock You paid for the tour. You didn't pay for conversation. (*Another clear of her throat*) Talk is extra.

George You don't miss a trick, do you?

Karen Look, William… I may call you William, may I?

Terry You may certainly not.

Karen Oh? Why?

Terry It's not my name.

Karen But you said…

Terry I said I was Shakespeare. I didn't say I was William. My name is Terry. Terry Shakespeare. William was my brother.

Karen (*disappointed*) Oh.

George That settles it, then. We're not paying good money to talk to Terry Shakespeare.

Olive But William's brother. I mean he must have known him mustn't he? He can tell us all about him.

Terry No.

Dilly What?

Terry I'm not saying a word about that bald-headed bastard.

Dilly Why not?

Terry I wouldn't be seen dead talking about bloody William. (*He begins to pace angrily about*) You are so gullible, you lot. You don't know, do you? You have no idea. Yes, I came here all those years ago. I worked all day and I wrote all night. I did. Not him. The complete works of Terry Shakespeare were penned in this very room. By me. And that slimy git came along and pinched the lot.

Karen William did?

Terry Of course he did.

Olive Fantastic.

Karen You mean to say, *Hamlet* and the rest ... they were written by you?

Terry No, no! *Hamlet*! That pile of garbage! The plays I wrote were better than that. He pinched my ideas and he ballsed them up—all the magic went out of them—the grovelling, two-faced little turd. Look, look, I'll show you. (*He runs back to the rubble and pulls out a pile of papers*) Look at this. My plays. *The Complete Works of Shakespeare.*

George Terry Shakespeare?

Terry Of course. I've got a whole series of plays about the kings of England here and it's bloody brilliant. All fights and adultery. I call it *The Fractions*.

Dilly *The Fractions*?

Terry Yes.

She doesn't understand

Richard the Third. Henry the Fifth. All that lot. And what does he do? For a start he gets rid of my title. And then he plods through the history. What possible use is that? Just think about it: a play about Henry, followed by another play about Henry, followed by another play about *another* Henry. And so on till we're knee-deep in bloody Henrys, none of them of the slightest interest. I mean, what would you rather see? His or mine? But do you get the chance? Of course you don't. My version was never performed. He saw to that.

Karen But why? I mean, why should he do that?

Terry He was a crook. I told the truth in my plays, and the truth hurts.

George The truth about William?

Terry Yes. Like the plays I did about our childhood. He couldn't stand them. (*He sorts through his papers*) Look, I'll show you. Here we are. One of my greats, this one is. *A Lot of Fuss About Very Little.*

Olive And you put William in this?

Terry I did. In fact, you can do a bit for me now. I haven't seen this done in centuries.

Mrs Craddock Just a minute. You're not performing plays in my attic. You'll need a license for that.

Terry I'm four hundred and sixty-five. I can do what I like.

Mrs Craddock You can if you pay for it.

Terry And how old are you?

Mrs Craddock Mind your own business.

Terry Don't be shy. (*He snaps his fingers*) How old are you?

Mrs Craddock Four. (*She is in some kind of trance and has become a toddler. She laughs and gurgles*) I'm four, I am. I'm a big girl.

George Good grief! What have you done to her?

Terry Nothing much. She's going to be in one of my plays, that's all. (*He fixes his eyes on Olive*) And so are you.

Olive Oh, no. Really. Actually I'm basically a backstage person...

*Terry snaps his fingers again and Olive also becomes a toddler.
She begins to cry*

    I don't want to be in a play. I want my mummy…

Terry Right. And I shall play the part of my little brother
William, aged three. This'll give you some idea of what a
boring kid he really was. (*He claps his hands*)

*They go into the scene. He finds an old swimming cap which he
puts on when he represents his bald brother. Mrs Craddock is
Toddler 1 and Olive is Toddler 2*

Toddler 1 What shall we play now?

Toddler 2 I know. Let's do mewling and puking?

Toddler 1 No. I'm fed up with that. Let's do something else.

Toddler 2 Let's play trains!

Toddler 1 They haven't been invented yet.

Toddler 2 Oh blow.

William I know!

Toddler 1
Toddler 2 (*together*) What?

William   Let's talk of graves, of worms, of epitaphs;
               Make dust our paper, and with rainy eyes
               Write sorrow on the bosom of the earth.

The others look at him a moment

Toddler 1 All right, then, let's play trains.

*They go chuffing off until Terry stops them with a clap of his
hands. They come out of their trance, a little dazed by the
experience*

Terry See what I mean? Spouting all that rubbish all the time.

Nobody understood a word he was saying. Least of all our old man. It used to get right up his nose. He had a little place in Stratford called Gloves-You-Like. He was down there all hours. After all, gloves were his life, and he liked to keep his hand in. Then he'd come home exhausted and find this bloody kid mouthing off all over the house. (*He sorts through his papers*) Now then. Here's another. *If You Fancy It.* (*He snaps his fingers*)

George and Karen become John and Mary Shakespeare

Come on, then, Mother. Let's have some grub.

Mary All right, Willy. Sit down nicely, then.

They sit on boxes, as if at a table, and Mary feeds Terry with an imaginary spoon. John approaches and sighs heavily

John What a day. We've been worked off our feet at the glove shop.

Mary Oh dear. Poor you.

John We're short-handed, that's the trouble. Stone me, but I could murder a mutton pie.

William Murder most foul, as in the best it is.

John What?

Mary Nothing, dear. He's just babbling.

John I've told him before about language at the dinner table. You watch your tongue, my lad.

William O wretched state! O bosom black as death!

John What did he say?

Mary There, there, Willy. Eat your prunes.

William Common Mother, thou, whose womb unmeasurable, and infinite breast, teems, and feeds all.

John Don't you speak to your mother like that. Bosom? Breast? Where does he pick up words like that?

Mary You know what the kids round here are like, John. Don't he too hard on him.

John I will not have him spouting filth when I'm about to eat. Listen to me, bugga-lugs, any more of that and you'll feel the toe of my boot.

William Sorry, Pa.

John I should think so. (*To Mary*) I don't know what we're going to do with that child, Mary, I really don't. He's not normal. Where did we go wrong?

Mary He's bored, that's all. He needs to go to school.

John Maybe you're right. School might knock all this crap out of him. It makes you think, though.

Mary What?

John How sharper than a serpent's tooth it is to have a thankless child.

Terry claps his hands and the scene ends

Terry Great last line, don't you think? He pinched that one complete, the sod.

Dilly But he was clever with words, wasn't he? I mean, he was bright.

Terry Bright my backside. You should've seen him at school. He was absolutely useless. (*He sorts through his papers*) Ah. This was a fantastic play. It's all about the old man's business difficulties, *Glove's Labour Costs*, and it has this scene which shows the little toe-rag at school. (*To Dilly*) And since you're so interested, you can be the teacher. (*He snaps his fingers*)

Dilly becomes a teacher. Terry sits on a box, writing. Dilly comes to look over his shoulder

Teacher Ah, Williamus. Let's see, let's see.

Williamus It's not very good, Miss.

Teacher I'll be the judge of that. (*She reads*) Oh, dearie me, Williamus. What's this supposed to say?

Henry Er... Where the bee sucks, there suck I, Miss.

Teacher And that's what you did on your holiday, is it? Following bees around?

Williamus No, Miss. I was using my imagination.

Teacher I should hope so. It's a most unhygienic thing to do. Your mother would have a fit if she thought you went around sticking your tongue in flowers.

Williamus Like I said, Miss, it was, you know, sort of imagination.

Teacher But, really, I didn't ask for imagination: I asked for a nice story. You must save your imagination for the upper school—when you do accountancy. And your spelling leaves a great deal to be desired. (*She points*) You don't spell "suck" like that, do you?

Williamus I think so, Miss. It's kind of Tudor.

Teacher Well, it's most confusing.

Williamus Yes, Miss. Sorry, Miss.

Teacher And what's this? "In a cowslip bell I lie." A cowslip bell, Williamus?

Williamus Sort of.

Teacher And where is this cowslip bell? On the way to school?

Williamus Not really, no...

Teacher No. Of course not. I think I might have noticed it if it were. A flower big enough for a great lump like you to lie in. I think I might have noticed that, don't you?

Williamus 'Spose so.

Teacher So this is what you think about in that bald head of yours, is it? Sucking where bees suck and climbing into flowers? Is it?

Williamus Well...

Teacher I don't think you're in any position to deny it, Williamus.
It's down here in black and white. So, tell me: what are you on?

Williamus On, Miss?

Teacher Come on, Williamus. I've been at this game too long to
miss the signs. (*She taps his work*) This stuff is either the
product of a diseased mind or you've been at the back of the
bike sheds inhaling something. Which was it?

Williamus (*mumbling*) A diseased mind, Miss.

Teacher What?

Williamus A diseased mind, Miss.

Teacher Then we'll have to put that right, won't we? (*She hands
him the work*) Do it again, and this time begin with "This year
we spent our holidays in Bournemouth" and carry on from
there.

Williamus But we didn't, Miss.

Teacher Neither did you spend them in a cowslip, but that didn't
stop you turning out this garbage, did it?

Williamus But I've never been to Bournemouth, Miss.

Teacher Then you'll have to use your imagination, won't you?

Terry claps his hands and the scene ends

Terry Useless, see. And he wasn't much better when it came to
games. We had this teacher called Mr Biggs who nearly bust a
gut trying to get my brother involved in sports. As you can see
from this scene from my great romantic tragedy, *Kevin and
Juliet.* (*He snaps his fingers*)

George becomes Mr Biggs, running on the spot

Mr Biggs Up two three! Up two three! Up two three!

Terry, as Kevin, also tries to run on the spot

And stop! That was, as per usual, Montagu, pathetic. What was it?

Kevin Pathetic, sir.

Mr Biggs You're not really interested, are you lad? You don't give a toss, do you?

Kevin I do my best, sir.

Mr Biggs Your best? Do you expect me to believe that that limp performance was your best? You great Mary-Ellen.

Kevin I think my talents lie in other directions, sir.

Mr Biggs And you needn't come the smart-arse with me, Montagu, because it won't wash. You can't be bloody bothered, boy. Half the time you don't even bring your kit.

Kevin But I always bring a note, sir.

Mr Biggs Yes, and it takes me thirty bleeding minutes to read it. Why can't you just say you've got a cold or something? Why do I have to wade through endless "forsooths" and "agues" and "soft what light through yonder window breaks"? You'll feel the light break round the back of your ear-hole if you try that on with me again. I'm a reasonable man but let's face it, laddie, you're crap at games. You're crap at cricket and you're crap at soccer...

Kevin Perhaps you haven't tried me in the right position yet, sir.

Mr Biggs Don't give me that. That bloody great turnip of yours is ideally suited to nodding in balls at the near post, but do you nod them in?

Kevin Not very often, sir.

Mr Biggs Not very often, sir. Which means once. An own goal. And when we tried rugby, what happened?

Kevin I was crap, sir.

Mr Biggs You were, indeed, crap of the least useful kind.

Kevin That wasn't my fault though. The others kept mistaking my head for the ball...

Mr Biggs Don't make excuses, son. We've tried you in every

sport known to man and it's the same story over and over again.
Running, swimming, bear-baiting…

Kevin We didn't have a proper bear, though, sir.

Mr Biggs Of course we didn't. What do you think this is: Eton?
You were supposed to be the bear.

Kevin I did my best.

Mr Biggs You were nothing like a bear, Montagu. More like a
bloody guinea pig. What kind of fun is that for the other lads,
eh? (*Menacingly*) Tell me, Montagu, what do you want to do
in life?

Kevin I was hoping to be a writer, sir.

Mr Biggs A writer? You soft tart. We'll soon put you straight on
that score, sunshine. Now, get moving. Up two three! Up two
three! Up two three!

Terry claps his hands and the scene ends

Karen You keep saying he was bald.

Terry He was bald. Everyone knows that.

Karen But not all his life, surely.

Terry Yes he was. Bald as a coot from the days of his childhood.
And he didn't like people mentioning it. It was a bit of a joke
in our family that you could never tell which way up young
William was. Of course, he never saw the funny side. As you
can see if you take a look at *The Merry Tarts of Streatham*. In
this one I've got Henry the Eighth quizzing his wayward wife,
Anne Boleyn. (*He snaps his fingers*)

George and Karen go straight into the scene, as Henry and Anne

Henry Nay, mistress; you take me for a lack-brain dotard.

Anne I do assure you, my liege, I have been faithful to you these
past two years.

Henry 'Tis not so! Give me the name of the traitor who dares to cuckold the king or it shall go hard with you.

Anne (*blushing*) It has already gone hard with me, my liege.

Henry Exactly! Hussy!

Anne Had you but known the man, sire——

Henry Tart!

Anne —as I have known him——

Henry What are you suggesting? I'll have your head off for this, you scrubber!

Anne It was Sir Roger. Of Wolverhampton.

Henry (*thrown for a moment*) Sir Roger?

Anne Aye, sir.

Henry The bald one?

Anne Aye, sir.

Henry (*mildly*) Oh. Well, see that it doesn't happen again.

Terry claps his hands and the scene ends

Terry You see? A pretty accurate picture of William, that. If you were bald, you were all right. Mind you, when it came to the local wenches running their fingers through his hair, he found himself at a distinct disadvantage. I explain all this in the famous casket scene from *The Estate Agent of Venice*. (*He snaps his fingers*)

We're straight into a sort of game show. Olive is Portia, George is the Prince of Majorca, and Dilly and Mrs Craddock are twinkling attendants. They find three caskets—lead, silver and gold—among the jumble and bring them forward. Terry plays Baldiano

Portia (*to the audience, waving and skipping about*) Surprise, surprise! Yes, it's me again, everybody: your old pal Portia with another round of "What's in the Casket?"

Audience reaction

> Now then, boys and girls, you remember what happened last
> week? That *luverly* Tony—wasn't he smashing, ladies—went
> off on a super trip to Egypt with his choice—Cleo! Unfortu-
> nately, Cleo ran into difficulties with her asp, and, well, poor
> old Tone took it rather badly and... Well, we don't want to go
> into all that, so let's find out... "What's in the Casket?" tonight!
> Bring on the first contestant, Anthea!

Attendant brings Majorca forward

> Now, butty, you know what you have to do, don't you, love?
> You answer my questions, but you mustn't say "yes" and you
> mustn't say "no". Understand?

Prince (*smugly*) I do.

Portia So, what's your full name, chuck?

Prince The Prince of Majorca.

Portia The Prince of Majorca! Oooh! How absolutely smashing!
Now then, belly button, tell me, you must drink a lot of wine on
Majorca. Am I right?

Prince You are, Portia. But I prefer a nice cup of tea.

Portia I bet you do, sauce-pot! And so do I. Mind you, I bet they
don't make tea like they do in Liverpool, do they?

Prince They don't, Portia.

Portia Did you know they use water straight from the Mersey,
and they don't strain it?

Prince I did not, Portia.

Portia Oh, yes, chuck. In Liverpool a lorra tea of Mersey is not
strained. Did you know that?

Prince I did not.

Portia You didn't say "no", did you?

Prince No.

An attendant gongs him out

Portia Oh, Prince! What a chuffer you are! Anthea's had to gong
you out. Never mind, ladies and gentlemen. He was a good
sport, wasn't he? Off you go then, eccles cake, and be sure to
give all our love to Majorca.

The Prince is led off, waving, and Baldiano comes forward

Ooh, this one's a sweetie, isn't he, boys and girls? What do they
call you, chuck?
Baldiano Well, Portia, sometimes they call me Flash and
sometimes they call me Fart-arse and——
Portia I mean, what's your name, butty?
Baldiano Oh, I see. Baldiano.
Portia Baldiano? That's a nice name. All right, then, Baldiano,
you know the drill?
Baldiano Yes.

Portia nudges him. She wants him to win

(*Suddenly realizing and adding*) —Terday I did. And I do now,
Portia.
Portia Oooh, Baldiano, you almost slipped up there, chuck.
You're not nervous, are you?
Baldiano No.

Portia nudges him again

(*Again realizing and adding*) —Tice the sweat on my brow. I
am a bit, Portia.
Portia Yes, I can see the light shining off the top of your head like
a beacon. OK, then, you've seen the notes on all these delight-
ful caskets. Which one are you going to choose?

Baldiano ponders. The others shout advice: Number two! Take the money! Open the box! etc. Eventually...

Baldiano I've made up my mind, Portia. I choose the gold...

She nudges him

The silver...

She nudges him

I mean the lead casket.
Portia You're sure, Baldiano, poppet?
Baldiano I'm sure.
Portia Then let's see what you've chosen! (*To an attendant*) Open the box, Anthea.

Tension as Mrs Craddock comes forward. She clears her throat. The box is opened. Baldiano looks in and is delighted

Well, well, well. He's done ever so well, ladies and gentlemen. Show us what you've got, Baldiano.

Baldiano is perplexed by this for a moment

In the box, love. Show us what you've got in the box. Oh, Baldiano! You've won tonight's star prize: a washable, drip-dry designer-label wig!

With a flourish, Baldiano takes a wig from the box. Applause all round. He tries on the wig. Terry claps his hands and the scene ends

Terry Of course, no-one ever performed *The Estate Agent of*

Venice. Bloody philistines. I didn't forget the basic quiz show idea, though. Some years later I offered it to the court of Queen Elizabeth as a winter entertainment which I called Bald Date, but it never quite caught on. But old William latched on to the wig idea all right. He came in for tea one day with a shifty look and a sudden profusion of flowing tresses.

Dilly Did it do him any good?

Terry Depends how you look at it. It was because of my wig idea that he managed to catch the eye of Anne Hathaway. Then, once he caught her eye, he went on to win her hand, and subsequently various other bits of her, too. You know how it goes.

Karen A good match, was it?

Terry Good for him. Anne ran a nice little tourist attraction just outside Stratford. Coach parties used to call for cream teas and a wander round the house, but until the arrival of old Baldy, no-one was quite sure what they were supposed to be looking at. Then all hell broke loose. You know: this is the great play-wright's house—how wonderful! Oh, look! This is his spoon—swoon, swoon! My God, this is where he hangs his tights! Fantastic! Me they ignored.

Olive So he was well known by this time?

Terry Oh, yes. By this time he was stealing my stuff hand over fist. And becoming famous for it. There's this poignant scene from my play *Everything's Fine If It Ends Up That Way.* It's about this bloke called Porker who's really pissed off with life, see, and he goes down the pub and tells the barmaid. You know, the way you do. (*He snaps his fingers*)

George becomes Porker and Karen becomes the Barmaid in a northern pub. She hands George a drink and wipes the bar

Barmaid Evening, Porker. How's tricks?

Porker Bloody awful, since you ask, Tracey.

Barmaid Oh? Why's that?

Porker Well, you know my old man just passed away?

Barmaid Hmm.

Porker He's come back as a ghost.

Barmaid (*not especially interested*) Oh dear.

Porker Came wafting through my front door last night. Tells me
it was my uncle who did him in——

Barmaid Tch.

Porker —and now he's shacked up with my mum.

Barmaid Your old man's shacked up with your mum?

Porker No, no. My uncle.

Barmaid With your uncle?

Porker No. You're not listening, Tracey. That's the trouble. No-
one really understands me. (*He drinks*) To be, or not to be: that
is the question.

Barmaid What?

Porker Whether 'tis nobler in the mind to suffer the slings and
arrows of outrageous fortune——

Barmaid I see, love.

Porker —or to take arms against a sea of trouble, and by
opposing end them?

Barmaid Well, it's bound to be a bit awkward at first, Porker.

Porker To die: to sleep——

Barmaid (*indicating the empty glass*) No more?

He nods and she begins to pull another pint

Porker And by a sleep to say we end the heartache and the
thousand natural shocks that flesh is heir to——

Barmaid 'Tis a consummation devoutly to be wished. I know,
love.

Porker To die——

Barmaid To sleep?

Porker To sleep perchance to dream, Tracey, love.
Barmaid True, Porker. Very true. You haven't seen my cloth, have you, cherub?
Porker (*pointing*) Ay, there's the rub.
Barmaid Thanks. Well, if you ask me, a nice nap could be just what you need.
Porker I'm not so sure, Tracey. I'm not so sure. For in that sleep of death what dreams may come——
Barmaid That's a point. I hadn't thought of it like that.
Porker —when we have shuffled off this mortal coil——
Barmaid Oh, don't take on so, Porker. Worse thing happen at sea.
Porker You could be right there, love, but, as it happens, my uncle has just booked me a passage on a boat.
Barmaid That's nice.
Porker What's his game, though? It must make you think. It must give us...

Pause

Barmaid What?
Porker Pause.

Terry claps his hands to end the scene

Terry (*wiping away a tear*) You see? All that pithy dialogue. But what did young William do? He pinched the lot, cut all the best lines and turned it into a soliloquy. He even changed Porker's name. Bloody ruined it.
Karen Well...
Terry No, he did. He took the pith right out of that scene. I said to him, I said, "You've turned poetry into dross, you utter fool!" But he wouldn't listen.

Karen To be or not to be, though. It is quite poetic in its own way, isn't it?

Terry Of course it isn't. It doesn't even rhyme! How can it be poetry if it doesn't rhyme?

Karen Well…

Terry No. You want poetry you do it like this. (*He snaps his fingers*)

George is Hamlet again

	Whilst others sought release in drink,

                Whilst others sought release in drink,
                Young Hamlet used to sit and think.

Hamlet I'm just not sure…

Terry —they'd hear him sigh——

Hamlet —whether it's best to live or die.
                It seems to take such nerve and pluck
                To put up with my rotten luck.
                Perhaps I should strike back at fate
                By dying and becoming late.
                And death is just like sleep——

Terry —he thought.

Hamlet Things really wouldn't seem so fraught
                If I dropped off—a pleasant scheme.
                Except, of course, that I might dream.
                Why put up with our awful life
                When we could end it with a knife?
                The trouble is that down that track
                Many may go but none come back.
                The future might cause much regret:
                The devil you know's a better bet.
                It's always been the same, I find:
                Start to think and you change your mind.

Terry claps his hands to end the scene

Terry *That* is poetry. But William wouldn't admit it. Oh no. He was the *writer*. He knew all about writing.

Olive So was he a proper writer by this time?

Terry Far from it. He was a journalist.

Olive On a newspaper?

Terry Exactly. He got himself a job on the local paper: *The Stratford Sun.*

Dilly He couldn't steal your material if he was working, though, could he?

Terry Don't you believe it. He took stuff straight out of *The Fractions* to put in the paper. (*He snaps his fingers*)

Mrs Craddock becomes a reporter with a notebook. The others call out the headlines

Group (*shouting headline*) A LOAD OF FRENCH BALLS!

Reporter (*brashly*) Newly crowned King Henry has just been presented with a gift. A couple of smooth-talking yes-men from the French Court delivered it yesterday. The gift, from the limp-wristed Dauphin, turned out to be a load of balls! Tennis balls, to be exact. Perhaps now the king will join the *Sun* in calling for the Frogs to be put firmly in their place.

Group (*shouting headline*) THE HOME FRONT!

Reporter And what a front, eh, readers! Saucy Stunna Mistress Quickly—see page three—says farewell to our brave lads. Here's a couple of points they might like to remember as they set off on their fantastic soar-away Frog-bashing tour.

Group (*shouting headline*) REJOICE! REJOICE! COWERING FROGS ON THE HOP!

Reporter England met France at Agincourt yesterday and the *Sun* is proud to bring our readers the result: England ten thousand; France twenty-nine!! And that's official! See page five for our cut-out frogs' legs. Wear 'em with pride!

Group (*shouting headline*) HERO HAL'S FRENCH DISH!

Reporter The man who crushed a crate-load of filthy foreigners at Agincourt has added one more frog to his list. This time he brought his trusty lance to bear on shapely Princess Katherine, busty daughter of the beaten Froggie King. A fairytale romance for Kath and Hal? We'll see. Perhaps a French kiss from Handsome Harry really will turn a frog into a true princess!

Terry claps his hands to end the scene

Terry That was all mine. He took the lot, stuck it in the paper, and then turned it into a play. There was no stopping him. Play after play he pinched. The last straw was this fantastic comedy I did called *Night*.

Mrs Craddock Which he also pinched?

Terry No because I kept it stuffed down the leg of my tights. But it flopped.

Dilly Down the leg of your tights?

Terry On stage. I did another version—*Second Night*—and that flopped. Then another and another, until I'd done eleven versions of the bloody thing. And then...

George Don't tell me.

Terry Exactly. The bald bastard strikes again. He wrote the next version and it was a smash. I was sick as a pig. I was so sick I never wrote another word.

Dilly That is really sad.

Terry Sad? It's a bloody tragedy. Nothing my brother wrote was a patch on *The Merry Tarts of Streatham*, and yet, who today has heard of Terry Shakespeare? No-one. It's just not fair. Well, I may be dead but I'm not stupid. I mean, I got the message: nobody wants me.

Dilly You mustn't give up, Terry.

George No. You've got such a story to tell. *My Life With William*.

Terry No.

Mrs Craddock If he starts writing up here again, that's work, that is.

Karen People have to keep body and soul together, Mrs Craddock.

Mrs Craddock He doesn't. And if he's working he's using my attic as an office. (*Another clear of her throat*) And that means office rates.

Terry I'm not writing any more.

Olive Why not? You could do a biography. *William Shakespeare—the Truth*.

Terry No.

Olive It could be a best seller.

Terry A what?

Olive Sell thousands of copies. Make a fortune.

Terry Really?

Mrs Craddock He'd need an agent. Fifteen percent...

George Fifteen!

Terry It's no use. I'm not writing about him any more. He gets enough publicity as it is. I'm sick of the sound of his name.

Karen Then perhaps you could write about something else.

Terry Like what? I'm out of touch.

Karen Television, radio, film...

George And if you don't want to write about William, you could do a thriller or something.

Olive Yes. Or crime.

Karen Yes. You could write for *The Bill*...

Terry I'm not writing for anything called that.

Karen But something. You could write something.

Terry Well...

Dilly Go on, Terry. You know you've got the talent.

Terry True, true...

Dilly The world deserves to hear your voice.

Terry Crime, you say? (*He begins to pace*) Let me see, let me see. There's this bloke, right? And he's amazingly talented...

Dilly Yes?

Terry And he has this brother who steals all his ideas and makes a packet.

All Yes, yes.

Terry And one day this bloke—the talented one—has had enough.

Olive "This has got to stop," he says.

Terry He does. But his brother is a mean bastard and he won't listen. So he bumps him off.

Olive Fantastic.

Terry The good guy murders the bad guy.

George What a twist! Brilliant.

Karen And the good guy is played by Mel Gibson.

Terry That's right. He is. But the police are after him. Even though he's the good guy.

Olive *The Drama Squad.*

Terry Yes, yes. *The Drama Squad.* Get me pens and paper.

Dilly and Olive scrabble around for pens and paper

Karen The police are on his trail. Inspector Hamlet of the Yard.

Terry Inspector Hamlet. I like it. And he's a mean bastard, too. A crook. Played by Alan Rickman. So the good guy has no choice. Hamlet has to go and he shoots him.

Dilly and Olive hand him the pens and paper

No. Not me. I'm creating. I dictate. You lot write.

In a fever of excitement, the others prepare to take down Terry's dictation

(*Pacing*) OK. So… Scene one. Interior. Stratford. Night. We see Mel Gibson sleeping. There are signs of strain on his handsome face. The door opens and this creepy bald guy sneaks in…

Karen Played by Boris Karloff…

Terry Yes!

George He's dead, isn't he?

Terry So what? I can arrange that. Boris goes to the desk and stuffs these sheets of paper down the front of his doublet. There is candlelight shining off the top of his head. Suddenly Terry—I mean Mel—wakes up. He grabs the candlestick and wham! Boris goes down in a pool of blood.

All Fantastic!

Terry Tremendous. This is going to be my greatest so far. This is going to make my name! At last!

Freeze on Terry in his moment of triumph, the others all poised to write. Music

CURTAIN

FURNITURE AND PROPERTY LIST

Further dressing may be added at the director's discretion

On stage: Chests
Old boxes. One contains a wig
Piles of clothes
Pile of papers
Old swimming cap
3 caskets—lead, silver and gold
Notebook
Pens and paper

Personal: **Dilly:** bag

LIGHTING PLOT

Property fittings required: nil
1 Interior. The same throughout

To open:	General lighting half up	
Cue 1	The door pushes open *A shaft of light from outside*	(Page 1)
Cue 2	**Olive**: "We might as well…" *Fade lights up fully*	(Page 1)

EFFECTS PLOT

Cue 1   To open   (Page
         Music

Cue 2   Voices are heard from outside   (Page
         Fade music

Cue 3   End of play   (Page 3
         Music